A Promise Made Is a Promise Kept

A Practical Guide for Strengthening Relationships
and
Having a Happy and Loving Marriage

BY

Matthew D. Jones Jr., LMSW, ACSW

iUniverse, Inc.
Bloomington

A Promise Made Is a Promise Kept
A Practical Guide for Strengthening Relationships and Having a
Happy and Loving Marriage

iUniverse books may be ordered through booksellers or by contacting:

iUniverse
1663 Liberty Drive
Bloomington, IN 47403
www.iuniverse.com
1-800-Authors (1-800-288-4677)

ISBN: 978-1-4620-2807-8 (sc)
ISBN: 978-1-4620-2808-5 (ebook)
ISBN: 978-1-4620-2809-2 (hc)

Printed in the United States of America

iUniverse rev. date: 6/3/2011

Contents

Acknowledgments

I wish to thank Elita St. Clair and Hattie Vanner
for their editorial assistance.

This book is Dedicated with Love and Affection
to my grandchildren

Elizabeth,

Phillip, and

Sarah.

Introduction

Deciding to marry is the most important decision a
person will ever make in his or her life. It will have
the greatest effect on one's personal growth. Why?
Because marriage is the only element in our life that can
give us the complete emotional, spiritual, and psychological
fulfillment of joy and peace. Decisions about education,
careers, homes, cars, vocations, and amassing material goods
are all about relatively short-term gratifications. Even when a
person has worked for the same company for thirty years or
more, the lifelong joy is not there after the job ends. One of the
ultimate goals most people have in life is to have a loving and
committed relationship that results in an enduring marriage.
However, strong marriages don't just happen. It takes many
years of hard work to have a lasting marriage. It can happen for
anyone who is willing to build a solid foundation with another
individual. Some couples make their relationship look easy, but
the best marriages require hard work. Love is not something
that should ever be taken for granted. It has to be constantly

nurtured and expressed. Although most relationships are a fifty-fifty arrangement with lots of give and take, marriage demands that each partner be prepared to give much more than he or she expects to receive in return. It is in the process of giving love and placing the needs of one's partner—rather than one's own needs—in the forefront that a person receives the gift of a loving marriage in return. Marriage is a sacred trust held by two people as they navigate together their individual lives and mold them into a shared life shaped by the celebrations and pleasures, as well as bumps and bruises, that are a part of every marriage. Most everyone who marries has high hopes and expectations for a meaningful marriage. While dating, we try to eliminate potential partners who just don't seem to have all that we want and need in a spouse. You meet someone who starts the adrenaline pumping, the eyes sparkling, and the dreams developing. High hopes and low maintenance keep the relationship humming along toward holy matrimony. You find yourself so in love that just hearing the other person's voice makes you melt, and it is obvious you are in the presence of a soul mate. Hours and hours of talking prove that this is the real thing, and poetic and profound words flow from your mouths. Love is wonderful.

But the journey to finding love and happiness begins during your childhood. The environment in which we are raised has the greatest effect on our future chances of finding love and happiness. As children we are exposed to a plethora of both positive and negative messages that adults create, either directly or indirectly. The messages come in the form of comments and behavior. The negative comments may include words such as *loser, weak, foolish, failure, hard headed, incompetent, crazy,* or *immature.* The positive comments may be phrases such as *you're smart, you're creative, you look good, you're dependable and mature.* Words of encouragement may include *I love you, great job, keep up the good work, and stay focused.* The positive behavior may take the form of hugs, kisses, playfulness, laughter, high-quality time together, and quiet moments together. Some examples of negative behavior are not giving hugs, yelling, shunning, very little emotional support, verbal put-downs, few kisses, and rejection. The point is that what happens during childhood either sticks to you or doesn't stick to you. Either way we grow up and carry those memories and experiences into our adult relationships. Many, if not all of those issues, will surface in our relationships. We often need professional help to decipher all the baggage if we had no one to talk with while growing up. The strain and the heavy baggage go into our adult relationships. Most people don't want to think about their baggage. They just want to think about how their mate makes them feel. Trying to understand ourselves as adults is challenging, but it's necessary if we want to have lasting and loving marriages. Understanding yourself starts with learning who you are as a person, particularly your self-concept—that is, how you view yourself—because it will determine how you experience life. If your experiences are positive and healthy, you will probably develop a positive and healthy life experience. If your experiences are shaky and fragile, you will find life's challenges overwhelming and sometimes insurmountable. Finding a good balance becomes our goal.

Looking at yourself from the standpoint of assessing your strengths, weaknesses, talents, and potential will assist you in learning to love and accept love on your terms in a healthy manner. You will be able to accept yourself as you are today despite your past experiences in some bad relationships. And you will know that you can improve any aspect of yourself that allows the sun to shine internally and externally in your relationships. Knowing yourself will create the ability to be honest with yourself and stay true to what you value, and to take full responsibility for your choices and actions.

Understanding yourself means that when you are in conflict with your partner, you can tune in to your disapproval of your partner's behavior or your lack of feelings, and sense whatever pain (fear, hurt, anxiety, or disappointment) is being covered up. In a conflict, you must first try to understand what you reacted to, and then explore why you reacted as you did. Getting to the bottom of your feelings and understanding them takes time, so please be patient with yourself. You will become more aware of what is inside of you, and you will begin to question why you feel the way you do about different things in your relationship. The more you understand, the more you can make changes in yourself and improve your relationship. The path to discovery is not always straight. If you keep paying attention to whatever exploration is going on and trust the feelings to lead you, you will eventually reach the awareness and peace you seek to have a winning life strategy. You have to be honest about where your life is right now. There is a connection between knowing precisely where you are in your life today and where you want your life to be.

When the demons from your childhood or past relationships appear, you will be able to recognize and deal with them so they do not affect your current relationship.

The purpose of this book is not to describe a pathological marriage but to define the nature of ordinary marital difficulties and show ways to improve your relationship. Once the various components of the problems have been exposed, couples can begin to talk about how they can solve the problems. There are a multitude of issues that can affect a marriage. I have chosen only a few. Some twenty years ago I facilitated premarital sessions for couples. The amazing thing about the sessions was that each partner learned things about the other that helped strengthen their relationship. The most recurrent issues with the hundreds of couples I have worked with over the years are the ones addressed in the book. The divorce rate is considered high by some standards, but thousands of people are still getting married each year because they still believe in love and the institution of marriage. However, in a practical and realistic sense, not everyone will find their soul mate and get married. Life is full of dreams, and we don't stop having dreams and goals because of a few shortfalls or setbacks in life. We keep pushing forward and learn to be a better person for love, relationships, and possibly marriage. Ideally this book will simply encourage couples to look at and explore issues in a different light. It is not going to solve every marital issue, but at least it will get couples to talk and to think about fighting for their marriage. My hope is that everyone who reads this book will take a deep inventory of who they are and who they want to become in this world.

That means confronting and learning to understand the fears, disappointment, hurts, and pain they have experienced in life. I hope they will come to the realization that the previous negative baggage does not make up who they truly are. I hope they look in the mirror each day and say to themselves, "I deserve better and will not stop until I reach my full potential and enjoy the wonderful treasure of a loving relationship with a man or woman whom God has prepared and created for me in this life." I strongly recommend that every couple participate in premarital counseling or premarital classes for at least ten sessions with an experienced clergyperson or a professional marriage coach or counselor, because there is so much each person needs to know about their partner, and people tend not to ask probing questions while dating. Sometimes people are not sure they really want to hear the answers to some questions about their partner. In premarital counseling sessions a neutral person helps couples explore very important issues that will affect their marriage. The negative baggage becomes exposed, discussed, and neutralized. Have a good and lasting marriage.

Chapter One
The Purpose of Marriage

The purpose of marriage is to be found in the acceptance of God's will that the covenant relationship of husband and wife, both made in the image of God, shall be an image of his covenant relationship with his people. Marriage is the supreme expression of the togetherness of man and woman. Changing the way we look at marriage will result in changing the way we look at our mates. When we come to see marriage as a covenant, we are able to love our spouses in ways and at levels we never expected. But we must do more than simply understand covenant; we must begin to articulate covenant promises on a regular basis. And more than simply talking the talk, we must walk the walk. By applying the principles of covenant on a consistent basis, our marriages will become stronger, deeper, and more fulfilling than we ever thought possible.

There are good marriages and there are bad marriages. The spectrum goes from heavenly accord to hellish discord.

However, all relationships, good or bad, have one common quality. Those partners who have a bad marriage have chosen—have actually contracted—to have a bad marriage. And even though they may protest their condition, they still make daily choices to maintain the miseries of their relationship.

Likewise, the partners who have a good marriage have chosen—have actually contracted—to have a good marriage. And they make daily choices to build their relationship into an even better one. The law of attraction says that like attracts like, and that an individual will go through life attracting the same kind of scenes, problems, and people until that individual changes (this means, of course, until the individual changes his or her behavior). By choosing to change your behavior you can choose to change your marriage. The couples who want to make choices, who are sufficiently eager to prove their relationship and are willing to modify their behavior, will have very satisfying marriages. I believe that two individuals in their unique long-term relationship, like everything else in life, will experience a change. The behavioral interactions that produce joys today may become obsolete with the passage of time or the development of circumstances. Therefore, it is important that couples become aware of the changes within themselves and their life together, and learn how to adjust so that the levels of satisfaction remain high and the marriage is successful and lasts forever.

Issues couples need to consider and discuss while dating that will help to decide if their marriage will work:

+ Religious beliefs

- Values, beliefs, and expectations
- Love versus compatibility
- Emotional openness versus integrity
- Personal exploration from birth to present relationship
- Maturity and responsibility
- Commitment and perseverance through life with examples
- Financial literacy
- The changing seasons of life, love, and personal growth

Chapter 2
Effects of Friends and Family

Exploring the Way They Affect Your Relationship

"I'm drained. I feel as if I'm splitting myself between my fiancé and my mother [or parents]." How many women have said this? When a couple meet at the altar to join hearts and lives, part of the vow they take is to forsake all others. The success of a marriage may hinge on how well they deal with issues that arise among those closest to them: their family and friends. When couples have been dating for a period of time and decide to marry, they need to have an in-depth discussion about the type of relationships each person has with family and friends and their level of influence. The people with the highest level of influence will have the greatest effect on the marriage, because they are the ones from whom the couple will seek advice and guidance as the relationship grows. Couples need to discuss how others affect their relationship. For example, parents will always have something to say about the couple, and that's okay; the problem comes when the husband or wife tries to incorporate certain comments or actions that are clearly opposite to what their partner has said or wants to do in the relationship. The partner needs to honor his or her spouse. If the couple disagrees about something, that's okay, but people should never try to override what their partners said and go along with what a parent is saying just because it sounds right. Animosity may set in, especially with men, who are likely to say, "I'm the man of my home, not your parents." Even people who like their spouse's parent may still reject the comments. Family and friends tend not to look objectively at the relationship. Having disagreements is healthy, and couples just have to continue communicating until they can reach a consensus about what to do. Another problem arises when a couple starts responding to what their friends are saying. A partner may seek insight from another married couple when there is an impasse on an issue. Couples should be wary of the comments from friends who are in unhappy relationships, are angry a lot, or have nothing good to say about their marriage. Couples should avoid any negative vibes from friends.

When couples have issues or concerns, they should seek out neutral people, because family members or friends will always be biased in their responses. Family and friends mean well when they offer or are asked for advice. Even if the partner is clearly wrong about something, they will consciously respond with the best interests of the family member in mind. If they tried to be objective, it would go a long way toward helping couples. When family and friends side with someone just because they are family, it does nothing to help the marriage.

Parents can be on the wrong side of an issue. I have seen this happen many times with couples, and it affects the marriage in a negative way. Well-meaning family and friends seldom ask about the other side of an issue; they are hearing only one side. Couples are able to work through any and all issues in their relationship if they just use all their listening skills and some common sense. They should try not to seek the advice from anyone who does not have the experience of being in a long-term, meaningful relationship; after all, you don't ask a plumber how to treat a toothache. Couples can always go and see a trained marriage coach, and they should surround themselves and interact with other couples who have positive energy to share about their marriage.

Couples face all types of pressure and challenges from family and friends. They're often asked when they're going to have kids, how they spend their money, what type of home they will live in, what kind of career choices they plan to make, and who makes the major decisions in the marriage. Couples need to show a united front in their marriage, especially in the face of any criticism. The kinds of questions mentioned above are generally directed toward couples who are young and married for the first time, although those married for the second or third time can experience the same or similar questions. It's important to remember that couples need to filter any and all comments made about their marriage. It's equally important for people to stand up and protect their mates when family or friends are badmouthing him or her unfairly. People have all sorts of reason to say negative things about one's mate. It's important to challenge some statements, especially if the statement is false or a character assassination. People will dislike other people for some of the silliest reasons, without any real validation. Couples must remember who married whom and why. You are the one who will live with your mate, and not anyone else. Positive words of wisdom, insight, and encouragement, lighthearted news, and affirmation should always be welcome and accepted by couples who work at creating a happy and successful love affair.

Things to practice:

- Be open, honest, and share negative comments that could hurt the marriage.
- Be supportive of your partner when he or she has to stand up to family and friends because of negative comments.
- Develop a defusing ritual about negative comments people make toward your partner.
- Always discuss things with your mate before talking with family and friends.
- Never allow your mate to be blindsided by comments people have made that you are aware of.
- Try to turn some comments that are made into jokes, because some people just can't help themselves. They also say some of the dumbest things because of their insecurities.
- Never repeat anything negative to your mate that others have said about them, unless you both can laugh about it.

Chapter 3
Intimacy (Sexuality and Emotions)

The Glue That Holds Relationships Together

An intimate relationship is a particularly close interpersonal relationship. It can be defined as enduring behavioral interdependence, repeated interactions, emotional attachment, and need fulfillment. Humans have a universal need to belong and to love, which is satisfied when an intimate relationship is formed. We have intimate relationships with the people to whom we are attracted, and whom we like and love. We have romantic and sexual relationships and intimacy with those we marry, to provide and receive emotional and personal support. Intimacy generally refers to the feeling of being in close personal association and belonging together. It is a familiar and very close affective connection with another person as a result of a bond that is formed through knowledge and experience of each other. Genuine intimacy requires sincere dialogue, transparency, vulnerability, and reciprocity.

The meaning and level of intimacy varies within relationships. Intimacy is considered the product of a successful seduction, a process of rapport building that enables parties to confidently disclose previously hidden thoughts and feelings. Intimate conversation becomes the basis for confidences that bind people together. Developing an intimate relationship typically takes a considerable amount of time—months and years rather than days or weeks. To sustain intimacy for any length of time requires well-developed emotional and interpersonal awareness. Intimacy requires the ability to be in an intimate relationship both as individuals and as a couple. Intimacy evolves through reciprocal self-disclosure and candor. And intimate relationships are more enjoyable and can survive considerable disagreements. Love is an important factor in physical and emotional intimate relationships. There are two types of love in a relationship: passionate love and compassionate love. With compassionate love, potent feelings diminish but are enriched by warm feelings and attachment, an authentic and enduring bond, a sense of mutual commitment, the profound knowledge that you are caring for another person who is in turn caring for you, feeling proud of a mate's accomplishments, and the satisfaction that comes from sharing goals and perspectives. In contrast, passionate love is marked by infatuation, intense preoccupation with a partner, strong sexual longing, thinking of ecstasy, and feelings of exhilaration that come from being reunited with the partner. Emotional intimacy is not the same as sexual intimacy. Sexual intimacy can take place with or without emotional intimacy, and emotional intimacy often does not occur within any kind of sexual context. Emotional intimacy is a psychological state that occurs when the trust level and communication between two people is such that it fosters the mutual sharing of each other's innermost selves; it is unbridled mutual self-disclosure. Sadly, the lack of emotional intimacy in relationships is common, and as a result we pay a heavy price. The effects of its absence can easily be witnessed in strained and failed relationships all around us, and in a larger context, they are reflected in the staggering divorce rates. In our most intimate relationships, we seek to feel wholly accepted, respected, worthy, and even admired in the eyes of our partners. We would like our relationship to be a comfortable place for us when we are weary, a place of compassion and support. Emotional intimacy is needed for these feelings to develop and continue, and when there is a lack of emotional intimacy, the relationship breaks down. One or both parties might even seek to have these needs filled outside the relationship, and this of course only makes matters much worse. So the question has to be asked, why is the quality so often missing from our relationships? Emotional intimacy is the glue that holds our unions together. Why do we seem to avoid it like the plague? The majority of people have difficulty practicing openness and allowing themselves to be vulnerable with someone. This may be particularly difficult for men, because of gender socialization. However, both sexes can struggle immensely with divulging how they really think and feel for fear of rejection of their true selves. We can be especially afraid to expose our real selves to someone whose opinion really matters to us, for fear of being criticized, laughed at, or seen as undesirable for our expression of who we authentically are by someone very close and important to us.

Though these are the people to whom it is hardest to reveal our inner truths, ironically these are the very people that we most need to do it with. Many people are shielded from emotional intimacy for so long, they have not developed adequate communication skills in the area of intimate disclosure. We lack the ability to verbalize our true emotional wants and needs to our partner. It might be difficult to find exactly the right words to communicate our feelings accurately. In fact, it might even be difficult for us to formulate our wants and needs to our own selves. We might struggle to get in touch with such a truthful place within, since we are not used to dwelling there. If we add the fear factor to lack of experience and skill deficits we have in this area, the absence of emotional intimacy in our relationships is really no surprise.

If we want to develop more emotional intimacy with someone, we need to become familiar with how we truly feel. How can we share our authentic feelings, wants, and needs if even we are not aware of what they are? The solution is to become consciously connected to the feelings we have pushed down and buried for so long. We need to explore our feelings more completely until they are well-known to us. We need to step away from the hectic world, find a quiet place, and just sit with ourselves. It may be difficult to switch off the mind's chattering and get quiet. The mind's chatter might be a valuable aid at the beginning point, in that its content can give us fast insights into our deeper self. The mind's commentaries that can inform us, the ones we ordinarily disregard or hardly even notice, can go something like this: "I can't let the softer side of me show or I might be seen as a pushover and may not be respected, or I might be taken advantage of. If I voice my true opinion and it's very different from my partner's, I'm afraid he/she will judge me, or maybe it means we are not right for each other." A very common one is "I don't feel good/deserving/smart enough for him/her."

We must start by observing these statements neutrally, without self-judgment. We can just let them teach us about what has been going on inside as we continue to take advantage of this wonderful source of information during our quiet times. We become more familiar with how we truly feel underneath the layers of feelings. We begin to see connections that have eluded us and realize, for instance, that we became a workaholic to avoid getting close in a relationship. We might use inappropriate anger or other damaging noncooperative attitudes to create distance within our relationship out of the fear of emotional intimacy.

Eventually we will want to move beyond the thoughts of the mind into a deeper place where we can address our feelings without mental interference. We can sit quietly. By closing our eyes and focusing mentally on a peaceful image, or repeating a soothing phrase, we can quiet our thoughts and focus solely on our feelings. We allow ourselves to experience all of our emotions fully, without retreat. This can be a very powerful yet difficult experience because our feelings of fear, anger, frustration, pain, and sadness might be very intense. In fact, we might be able to remain engaged in this state for only a short period of time at first. It is an exercise that takes practice and patience, but it is crucial to the knowledge and growth of our inner selves, and that is crucial to our intimate relationships. Once we have begun to know our inner selves, how does this translate into emotional intimacy within our relationship? We need to consciously create the environments and opportunities for emotional intimacy to be present. It is essential that changes be made in the necessary areas to allow for the development of bonding time with our partner. As we become more aware, we can make changes accordingly. Without emotional intimacy you are walking a path of probability that may lead to the disturbing statistic of a failed relationship. Spend time with your partner each day. Set aside at least half an hour daily and begin to talk from the place of your authentic self. As you do so, you begin to experience being more vulnerable with each other. At times you may wish to be in each other's company in complete silence. This nourishes a more profound connection at the level of the soul and is an incredibly powerful builder of intimacy. The other form of intimacy is physical. Physical intimacy is sensual proximity and touching. It can be enjoyed by itself or be an expression of feelings (such as close friendship, love, and sexual attraction). Physical intimacy includes being inside someone's personal space, holding hands, hugging, kissing, caressing, and sexual activity. Physical intimacy is a natural part of human nature. Research has shown it has health benefits as well. When we hug, kiss, or touch, our bodies release dopamine and serotonin, which reduce the levels of stress hormones. However, a lack of physical intimacy can lead to feelings of loneliness, stress, and anxiety.

Having really good sex is not only fulfilling but can also leave you feeling empowered. Women can feel totally confident and full of feminine power after making love. For example, having sex the night before giving a presentation at work allows a woman to feel taller and more competent the next day. A woman needs to tell her husband exactly where she wants him to touch her and encourage him to take over the bawdy conversation. She can let him describe his favorite place on her body and tell her what he wants to do to her in vivid detail. A few choice words are the perfect confirmation to let him know when he's getting it right. She'll be sure to get an instant replay. Sexuality is ever changing. What couples start out with sexually at the beginning of the marriage will change. The question is what it will change into. For example, the husband may want to have sex one to four times per week initially, and his urge may increase or decrease over time. He may be satisfied with just one sexual position early on but want to try different positions later. He may develop a taste for pornography or start having fantasies. He may desire oral sex. Sexuality can take many forms for him. The same can be said for the wife. Some women do not reach their sexual peak until they are past thirty-five or forty years old. And a woman's sexual needs may change. Her need for sex may increase significantly. She may discover a desire to include sex toys. She may want to have oral sex or experiment with a fetish. The issue is how couples adjust as their sexual intimacy changes. If the partners did not have an in-depth discussion about their sexuality at the beginning of the relationship, there may be some problems. But the problems are solvable as long as the communication about their needs continues to be open and honest. However, if the couple does not communicate with sincerity, there will be problems that could lead to stress and complications, and threaten the relationship. There are many ways for both partners to be creative and be fulfilled sexually, and allow the marriage to grow intimately. Couples need to remember that age has nothing to do with sexual intimacy as you grow old gracefully together. Couples need to work and find a happy medium regarding their sexual needs. Both men and women need to take the time to say nice things to each other. Childbirth is a very important event that may change a couple's intimacy. Some men report that the intimacy cools down or stops altogether after a baby is born. Some women are more interested in being a mother than in being a wife. That kills the atmosphere, and sexual intimacy is shoved aside. Continued communication is a must during these times in the relationship.

Couples need to work at verbalizing and sharing their thoughts and feelings more. Women have to be sincere and tell their partner he still looks good and smells nice, his body is still hot—simple things that will put him at ease. A loving relationship must allow daily conquests; the game of seduction is crucial. Even if you have kids or a job and you're tired, always try to treat your husband like he's the same one you decided to spend the rest of your life with. The question is often asked, why does everything eventually end up having something to do with sex? It is simply because once some of our basic needs are met, the first thing we think of is sex—even before wealth, and vacations. Even homeless people who may not know where their next meal is coming from think of sex. The reason we all crave it and feel great when we get it in the right amount is that it has both a physical and emotional effect on us. And many studies have proved that sex is good for our health and overall well-being.

Activities to practice to sustain sexual intimacy:

+ Try sex in the shower.
+ Go shopping together for a sex toy.
+ Create more intimacy by touching more, kissing, holding hands in public, and giving massages.
+ Get rid of the TV in the bedroom.
+ Try role playing.
+ Make love in different parts of the home and try different positions.
+ Try to take a quarterly short weekend trip together one to four hours away from home.
+ Have date nights.
+ Try phone sex as a prelude or send sexy text messages to each other.
+ Women need to learn the Kegel exercise (in which one contracts and controls the pelvic-floor muscles) to enhance sexual stimulation.
+ Have a passion for life's sexual journey and for the process required to go from boring to bliss in the bedroom.
+ Become dedicated to mutual pleasure.
+ Perfect the ability to communicate openly and honestly your most secret sexual desires and needs.
+ Have the keenness of mind to recognize the value of making love versus only having sex.

- Be willing to be a student of great sex; read about it, study it, practice it.
- Learn to be intentionally spontaneous and open to the opportunity to make love anywhere safe.
- Cultivate the generosity to consider your love partner's pleasure before your own.
- Ask for the variety of pleasure you want and deserve.

Chapter 4
The Role of Money

How Money Can Determine the Focus of a Marriage

If you and your partner have had an argument lately, chances are it was about money. Surveys show that finances put a huge strain on relationships. One of the reasons is that many people are attracted to their financial opposite. I have heard about all sorts of situations in relationships, from domestic dictatorship, with one partner controlling all the money, to financial infidelity, in which one partner thinks nothing of hiding purchases. Some couples live in a state of financial anarchy. Without checks and balances one partner may spend and accumulate debt while the other partner saves. Fortunately, falling in love with your monetary opposite doesn't have to be toxic. Even if one of you is a saver and the other is a shopaholic, you can find a middle ground so you don't end up wanting to throw all those shoes at each other. All couples need to have a serious discussion about their financial values while they are still dating. Money is a fundamental issue in marriage, and you'd like your values to match. Even couples whose money styles mesh need to clarify the way they will handle finances. There was a time when couples took for granted that they would have a good financial future, with the husband as the primary breadwinner. Now both partners usually have full-time jobs. Some couples need to treat their finances like a corporation. Create an income statement and a balance sheet so you can look at what comes in and what goes out every month.

When it comes to managing money, 90 percent of it has to do with your psychological makeup rather than your actual financial know-how. And just what are those psychological roots? For many, they begin in childhood. A number of partners are hesitant and uncertain about finances. Many watched their father handle the bills and their mother take care of the home, so they don't see themselves as good financial decision makers. Some partners top off a bad day at the office with an indulgent splurge without truly understanding what motivates them to spend money. In some cases, it's a quest for immediate gratification to ease emotional wounds. They may also have a sense of hopelessness, a feeling that they will never have enough money to do anything with, so they might as well spend it. Then there are those who deprive themselves in favor of taking care of others. Now that more women are graduating from college and in the workforce, the financial balance of relationships has changed. Many men have a problem dating or marrying women who make more money than they do, because some women use it as a weapon to make men feel inadequate. Some men see a high-achieving woman as a threat to their masculinity, creating a question about who will have the most power in the relationship. That is a no-win scenario, because a relationship set up as a power struggle will experience problems regardless of who brings in the most money. Education is potentially divisive, too, because it may raise the issue of class. Sometimes a man may feel inferior or inadequate when he's with a more educated woman. And one of the hardest situations for a man to handle is feeling useless because of his education to his woman. Not that the relationship is impossible, but it takes extra sensitivity on her part. It also requires a deep appreciation for the man inside, not just his accomplishments. And that is what the best relationships are built on.

It is ideal for couples to discuss and work through financial matters well before they make wedding plans, because when the officiant pronounces them man and wife, that includes any and all debt. Living happily ever after means talking openly and honestly about financial issues and agreeing on spending priorities.

Ways to face challenges and avoid money problems:

+ Discuss financial goals individually and as a couple, including those concerning career, education, homeownership, and so on.
+ Develop a plan of action to accomplish your goals.
+ Review the plan every month or annually.
+ Discuss how you will do your banking. Consider whether you will have one account, two separate

accounts, an account for bills, another for vacation, and so on.

+ Develop a plan to enjoy your money together—for example, vacations, cars, and donations to charity.
+ Agree to not make any purchases above a certain amount without talking it over with each other.
+ Discuss together how you will respond to friends who ask either of you for a loan.
+ Agree that both partners will sit down to review your financial state. If this is the second or third marriage for either of you, discuss how past finances were handled—i.e., wills, trusts, scholarships, and so on. If there are other children and grandchildren and money has been put aside for them or for a special interest, how will you handle it going forward? Do you discuss finances only in terms of when the two of you became a married couple?
+ Discuss the what-ifs: loss of job, major emergencies, illness, and so on.
+ Develop an emergency fund.
+ Discuss life insurance.
+ If either of you has children already, discuss how spending and saving will change if the two of you have children together.
+ Discuss how to use any money you receive unexpectedly.

Chapter 5
Children

Looking at the Role Children Play in a Marriage

Most people who are in a committed relationship would like to have children after marriage. Some couples may have children from previous relationships. Children can simply add more joy to a relationship. However, for the marriage to continue, there must be some basic and fundamental ground rules and understanding about the children. If there is not a good understanding about how to raise children, the relationship is headed for trouble, especially if they are very young or adolescents. Children can cause couples to divorce—not because the children are being themselves, but because the parents did not develop a game plan for how to be good and loving parents to all of them.

The first thing couples need to do is discuss their philosophy about raising children—every aspect of it. For example, discipline, what is appropriate for a girl or a boy, rewards, modeling behavior, ways to show affection, expressions of love , chores, school, sports, entertainment, friends, family interactions, and giving individual and group attention. Other aspects to discuss include changing behaviors, what happens when kids try to play parents against each other (especially if they have different parents), acceptable styles for boys and girls, religious teaching, and house rules and standards. In addition to the above it is critical that couples discuss the appropriate response when children are living in more than one home—in other words, the drama that happens with the ex-wife or ex-husband. Many people struggle to be a mature and rational adult when it comes to their child living or spending time with another adult. And some parents try to sabotage new relationships through the kids. If children are dividing their time between two homes, it is a must for parents to present a united front to the children. Parents must set realistic boundaries and be very persistent and consistent with the children about the expectations of behavior in the home. It is important to remember that all children want to be part of a secure, loving, and nurturing home regardless of who is playing the role of parent. Ideally, when there are children from a previous relationship, the new relationship partners will sit down together with the children and share what is expected in terms of behavior in their home. Keep in mind that the behaviors will vary based on the age of the child. And don't have just one sit-down talk; have a regular discussion weekly, because situations and circumstances change and behaviors are in a constant stage of fluctuation. Change will help the new relationship grow if done right.

Parents whose partners have children from previous relationships must have a ton of patience and learn flexibility, because children need time to grow into a new relationship with new adults. New parents must openly express their love and firmness toward the children and realize that the children may reject them periodically. This can be handled with love, affection, affirmation, needed discipline, and open communication. Remember, children are concerned about their role in the new relationship and will take action to maintain the status quo. They will struggle to retain a familiar and predictable environment, although they may seek to resist the improvement of a new relationship. The family is a system, and all systems tend to resist change unless all parts of the system participate in the change.

Some children may be in the home full time and some may be part time. Parents remain parents to each and every child who comes into the home. Blended families aren't for wimps. You can't be selfish and needy in a mixed family. A former patient said, "I was very naive. I thought I could slip and slide into the relationship. I already had two children. What were three more? Of course I would care about them and love them. We didn't sit down with our eyes wide open. It was very difficult in the early years. If I had to do it over, I would certainly do things much differently. Like looking at all aspects of what a blended family really means and the importance for parents to take a very strong unified stance when communicating with and about the children and birth parents."

The goal of blending families is to deeply understand that this family will never be a first family. It's always going to be a blended family that includes ex-spouses, previous history, and different values. People don't realize what this means. In their hearts and souls many people think, "I'm going to have this man or woman all to myself." But wait a minute. The children are there, and they start acting out their own losses and resentments in this new situation, because they didn't get to vote on this new relationship.

The most important predictor of a blended family's success is that the new couple has a strong, committed, bonded, and healthy relationship to stabilize the new family. In blended families, couples have to develop good coping skills. It is healthy for couples to connect during the day, sharing events about the kids, laughing, and having some physical intimacy. It's easy for comments like "Your children are nasty" or "Your negative ex-spouse called today" to add drama in a relationship. There are multiple potential stressors from an ex-spouse, including resentment and jealousy. Couples who connect daily send a supportive message to each other. It models a strong relationship and helps them feel secure. Different styles of child rearing, including discipline, can be frequent points of contention in a blended family. Stepparents have to develop a relationship with their partner's children, and the children have to develop a relationship with the stepparent. Gently, and with passion, parents have to get to know the children and build trust. Once you build a trusting relationship, parenting can be much easier and children can appreciate different parenting styles. There can be a great deal of anger, hostility, and resentment from an ex-spouse because of the new relationship. You want to accept the fact that the ex-spouse is just that: an ex-spouse. You're the one with the wedding ring and in a loving relationship. Time is on your side. You need to work on yourself and be a mature and flexible person who can work toward being able to respect and include all the children in a loving family.

Ways to practice good parenting:

+ Let the children see you being physical with each other—kissing, touching, and hugging each other affectionately.
+ Let the children hear you tell your partner, "I love you" daily.
+ Have daily family discussion about what's going on and how the children are adjusting.
+ Show a united front with the kids at all times.
+ Never disagree in front of the kids about something one partner told the children to do.
+ Each partner must make a habit of spending time with the other's child(ren) weekly.
+ Encourage the children to talk openly and honestly about their concerns in the family.
+ Never openly show any favoritism toward any of the children, especially your own, unless they have special needs.
+ Allow the children to have *some* say about decisions made in the home.
+ Each partner must openly and sincerely say, "I love you" to the children individually on a daily basis.
+ Have a family night where you play board games.
+ Have an all-female or all-male night out together.

+ Let the children know that the parents will always check with each other before decisions are made granting any request, to avoid playing the partners against each other.
+ Go over the expectations for each child in the home.
+ Try to eat dinner together as often as possible and talk about the day's events with everyone.

Chapter 6
Handling Problems

A Right Way and a Wrong Way

Disagreements are inevitable in a marriage. But a difference of opinion can easily escalate to verbal abuse if one partner begins to attack the other person instead of the problem. Everyone brings issues to a relationship stemming from things that happened years ago and can affect the relationship. Everyone has a secret cache of private wounds. Nobody has life all sewed up, and having issues doesn't mean we're doing life wrong. Realizing that each person has a small corner of the pain in the universe helps us feel less isolated. It doesn't negate the pain or issue, but it makes it a shared experience. It should make you more compassionate with your mate. Remember, your partner did not cause the pain. Couples must decide not to stay angry or stuck in past situations that caused the pain in their life. Anger is like an explosion in the mind. We have to wait until the clouds of dust settle before we see what the next move should be, and before we know how to respond and help our spouse overcome the pain and begin to heal.

It's a normal protective reflex for some people to get agitated or upset in the moments of a heated disagreement. But they don't have to stay angry. It is important to take a stand and correct situations that cause pain. It's also important to ask yourself how you can move on. You don't want to remain in an agitated mood, to continuously revisit and enshrine that moment of pain. You must move forward. Anger, blame, and resentment make people feel scared at heart. People have a choice of remaining in a belligerent state of anger, bound by their past, or moving forward. Past conditioning colors our view of current relationships, and it can be challenging to separate that past emotional template from the current experience. It just feels real. We can't get rid of our templates, but we can pay attention and recognize them. These are the glasses through which I can see the world today. As the world and your relationship continue to change, you must change the glasses through which you see. A mentor once told me that common sense wasn't so common. If it was, we would likely handle conflicts in our relationship much differently from how we usually do. Winning the argument in many instances seems to take priority over the well-being of the relationship or the feelings of our loved ones. The way we treat those we love the most doesn't make sense, and it's a fact of life that conflicts occur.

The way we handle conflicts can make all the difference in the world. Couples cannot pick at every little mistake that their partners make. Doing so will eventually build layers of resentment in a relationship. Everything your partner does should not be a serious issue. People need to decide what's important and what's not important in their relationship.

Forgetting to take out the garbage does not mean that he is lazy, and being late for an engagement does not automatically indicate that she does not respect his time. If you constantly point out every fault or mistake your partner has made, your interactions will soon turn into mere finger pointing. Instead, talk about the positive aspects of your relationship and what both of you can do to fix any problems. Remember, you don't have to have the last word. When couples talk constructively about their differences, amazing things happen in their relationship. They become stronger and healthier as a result of determining solutions to problems together. The focus is on nurturing and growth instead of placing blame. Pride and egos drive us into wanting to win and get the upper hand and be victorious in our arguments, but in the end, being right is small consolation when we end up alone.

Ways to practice problem solving:

- Develop good listening skills.
- Develop a fair way to communicate problems.
- Agree to discuss problems using a point-by-point process, which means listening and responding only to the stated point.
- Agree to not feel sensitive when problems are brought up.
- Agree to not let problems simmer.

+ Agree to come up with a solution for each problem discussed on the same day and not wait until another day.
+ Agree to not repeat old stuff.
+ Agree to put yourself in the shoes of your partner to better understand his or her concerns.
+ Agree to never minimize your partner's concerns.

Chapter 7
Trust and Forgiveness

The Foundation for Growth

Trust is the foundation for intimate, secure, and successful relationships. It must be earned and maintained with consistent actions. But building trust and feeling like one's partner is trustworthy are not always easy for those who have had their trust betrayed in the past. Trust has to be a living, breathing entity for a relationship to survive.

Trust means to believe. "I trust you" means I have no doubt in my mind about your honesty, integrity, and credibility. Relationships cannot survive without trust. Developing and keeping trust in a relationship is critical, because when the trust breaks, the relationship breaks. If you don't trust a person, you may still love them, but your relationship will not survive. Every relationship starts with trusting each other. Without the initial trust, the relationship will not move in the beginning. In the beginning, one believes without much proof that they can trust the other person. However, behaviors will determine how trustworthy the person is or will become. As the relationship grows, issues start forming because of doubts about whether the other person can be trusted. One asks oneself, was the other person trustworthy from the beginning or was I fooled? Or is the person changing now? This kind of doubtful thinking causes tremendous strain in a relationship, and with the breaking of trust, the relationship may end.

How you manage to build trust in the beginning is most important, because the beginning of a relationship can be very shaky. What may arouse suspicion should be avoided at all cost. If you have a suspicious partner, you need to communicate better. Small things such as going out with friends can be an issue. If there is a change in your mood, talk to your partner about the reasons for the change. If you are facing career problems, rather than hiding them, tell your partner and seek support. Sometimes, people act differently when facing career issues, and it may make their partner feel insecure. Be open about everything. Your words and body language should be in sync at all times. Inform your partner about everything, and if you are under pressure, be open. Seek trust and you will receive it.

Intimacy cannot exist without trust, and trust needs three things to exist: safety, honesty, and respect.

Simply put, intimacy and trust go together. In order to be intimate physically, emotionally, and spiritually, individuals have to let their guard down and be authentic and genuine.

This requires a sense of emotional safety on both sides, and a belief that one's partner will not betray or intentionally hurt the other. There are some core elements of trust. Trust is built on a foundation of emotional safety. The world can be a chaotic and scary place, yet the environment of a marriage should be safe. Trust is still a sensitive issue for many people. Couples can focus on some areas to help create a sense of comfort, peace, and safety for themselves and their partner.

We often think of forgiveness as something that someone who has done us wrong must ask of us. There is always another way of looking at it. My belief about forgiveness suggests that you focus on offering forgiveness to the person who has wronged you. To not forgive them is like taking a poison—continuing to suffer for what they did or didn't do to you—and expecting them to die. Forgiveness is an act of the imagination. It dares you to imagine a better future, one that is based on the blessed possibility that your hurt will not be the final word on the matter. It challenges you to give up your destructive thoughts about the situation and to believe in the possibility of a better future. It builds confidence that you can survive the pain and grow from it. Telling someone how you feel is a bonus, but it is not necessary to begin the process to heal the pain. Forgiveness has little or nothing to do with another person, because forgiveness is an internal matter.

Choice is always present in forgiveness. You do not have to forgive, but there are consequences. Refusing to forgive by holding on to the anger, resentment, and a sense of betrayal can make your life miserable. A vindictive mind-set creates bitterness and lets the betrayer claim one more victim. One misconception about forgiveness is that forgiving the offense, such as an affair, means that you condone it. Not true. In fact, we can forgive only what we know to be wrong. Forgiveness does not mean that you have to reconcile with someone who treated you badly. Another misconception is that it depends on whether the person who did you wrong apologizes, wants you back, or changes his or her ways. If another person's poor behavior were the primary determinant for your healing, then the unkind and selfish people in your life would retain power over you indefinitely. Forgiveness is the experience of finding peace inside and can neither be compelled nor stopped by another person. I believe that to withhold forgiveness is to choose to remain a victim. Remember, you always have a choice. When you forgive, you do it for yourself, not for the other person. The person you have never forgiven ... owns you. "What about the affair?" you ask. Just because you choose to forgive does not mean you have to stay in the relationship. The choice to forgive is always yours.

When you feel forgiveness is necessary, do not forgive for the other person's sake, but for yourself. It would be great if the person came to you and asked for forgiveness, but you must accept the fact that some people will never do that. That is their choice. They did what they did and that is it, except for the consequences, which they must live with. The hurt won't heal until you forgive. Recovery from wrongdoing that produces genuine forgiveness takes time. For some, it may take years. Don't rush it. Constantly reliving your wounded feelings gives the person who caused you pain power over you.

Instead of mentally replaying your pain, it helps to focus your energy on the healing, not the pain.

Compassion is one of the key ingredients of forgiveness. Learn to look for and appreciate the love, beauty, and kindness around you. You may have to change your thinking and behavior to discover compassion. To have compassion for others, you must first have compassion for yourself. Healthy, loving relationships are not possible without forgiveness. You cannot have a loving or rewarding relationship with anyone else, much less yourself, if you continue to hold on to things that happened in the past. Regardless of the situation, make peace with past love partners, parents, children, bosses, or anyone whom you think has done you wrong. The only way to improve your chances of having a healthy relationship with yourself and others is through forgiveness.

It is not possible to truly be present and available to a new relationship until you heal the pain and hurt of the past. Forgiving someone else means agreeing within yourself to overlook the wrong they have committed against you and to move on with your life. It's the only way. It means cutting them some slack. "What?" you say. "Cut them some slack after what they did to me? Never!" Let go. Move on. Nonforgiveness keeps you in an internal struggle. Being willing to forgive can bring a sense of peace and well-being. It lifts anxiety and delivers you from depression. It can enhance your self-esteem and give you hope.

Forgiveness is a journey. You may never forget, but you can choose to forgive. You can forgive, and tomorrow you may feel the pain all over again. As life goes on, you may choose to remember and feel the pain, and that is the time to once again remember that you have already forgiven. Mentally forgiving again is necessary. Then move forward. When we allow it, time can dull the vividness of the memory of the hurt, and it eventually fades. Always remember that you are important. Sometimes people do and say hurtful things. It is important to focus on what you have done to learn from the experience.

Forgiveness is a creative act that changes us from prisoners of the past to liberated people at peace with ourselves. It is not forgetfulness, but it involves accepting the promise that the future can be more than dwelling on memories of past pain. There is no future in the past. You can *never* live in the present and create a new and exciting future for yourself and your partner if you are always stuck in the past. Begin again. It is truly impossible to start anew and make clear, healthy, life-giving choices until we have let go of past pains, confusion, and resentment. Old wounds have a drawing power and pull our attention to them over and over, taking energy and hope from us and preventing us from starting again. Old wounds raise fearful specters of the same thing happening again in the future. For this reason it is important to spend time understanding the true nature of forgiveness and what it really entails. To forgive means to give up, to let go. It also means to restore oneself to basic goodness and health. When we forgive, we are willing to give up resentment, revenge, and obsession. We are willing to restore faith not only in ourselves but in life itself. The inability or unwillingness to do this causes harm. Remember, forgiveness can lessen the grip of pain on you and help you focus on the positive part of your life. Forgiveness can even lead to feelings of understanding, empathy, and compassion for the one who hurt you. However, forgiveness doesn't mean that you deny the other person's responsibility for hurting you, and it doesn't minimize or justify the wrong. You can forgive the person without excusing the act. Forgiveness brings a kind of peace that helps you go on with life. Letting go of grudges and bitterness makes way for compassion, kindness, and peace. Forgiveness can lead to

+ healthier relationships;
+ greater spiritual and psychological well-being;
+ less stress and hostility;
+ lower blood pressure;
+ fewer symptoms of depression, anxiety, and chronic pain; and
+ a lower risk of alcohol and substance abuse.

It's very tempting to imagine that when you meet the right person, you will immediately be able to trust him or her completely. Not so. Genuine trust is always earned, and it must be earned from three directions. You must be able to trust yourself, you must be a trustworthy partner, and you must discover the extent to which your partner can be trusted.

It takes personal insight to determine if you can trust yourself in a new relationship. You are tested to see if you will show up and take your claim for what you need, how you feel, and what you want to see changed in yourself. You also see your own weaknesses and limitations, where you need to grow and develop, and what the relationship needs from you if it is going to make it.

Ways to practice and maintain trust and forgiveness:

+ Spell out your expectations in the relationship.
+ Review your own expectations regularly.
+ Learn to be patient with each other's personal growth.
+ Have ongoing discussion about trust and forgiveness and your sensitivity to trust.
+ Talk about the past, but don't harp on it all the time.
+ Learn to forgive and release the negative feelings to a higher power.
+ If trust is violated, try to consider the whole person, not just their one behavioral mistake.
+ Learn to make concessions.
+ Be predictable with positive behavior.
+ Inform your spouse when you become unpredictable.
+ Make sure your words match the message. Mean what you say and say what you mean.
+ Do not keep any secrets.
+ Let your needs be known.
+ Look at your own behavior before pointing a finger at your spouse.
+ Remember, there is no love without forgiveness, and there is no forgiveness without love.

+ Sincere forgiveness isn't colored with expectation that the other person will apologize or change.
+ Follow through on promises.

Chapter 8
Boredom

Don't Let It Affect Your Marriage

As shared by one woman, "When we were dating, he was the most attentive and romantic man I had ever met. He'd go out of his way to make sure we spent plenty of time together, and he made it a habit of telling me I was the most important person in his life. We'd be out window-shopping, and he would suddenly spin me around and give me a long kiss as if he didn't care who was watching. I had never felt so emotional and spiritually connected to another person. Now all that's pretty much gone. Not long ago he started shutting down. He's not angry; he just doesn't seem interested in me anymore. We don't go out, don't make love unless I push for it, and no matter how often I ask him what's going on, he doesn't have an answer. We're like roommates." This may sound familiar to a lot of women in relationships. And they all ask the same question: what happened and when?

The short answer is that after some men get married, they feel like they have won the prize and conquered in the chase and now they can just cruise. Gradually boredom may set in and the intimacy becomes less and less. The challenge is that although men value intimacy as much as women do, they simply differ dramatically in their view of what it takes to achieve and maintain it. For men, intimacy is a prize to be gained by getting to the finish line in strict sequential order and with minimal repetition. The linear progression goes something like this: (1) express interest; (2) date to build trust; (3) make a commitment. You've got each other now. Once a man has moved to the next level of closeness, he finds no practical value in maintaining the traditions associated with the previous level. Men see intimacy as a settled fact, an achieved good that implies they no longer need to do what they have already done to gain it. For some men, repeating earlier expressions of intimacy ("Why are you asking me if I love you when I told you a long time ago that I do?") suggests to him that the two of you really haven't made it to the finish line. It's like having to repeat a grade in school. Added to this is the reality that intimacy is a completely subjective feeling of closeness. For women it often means, "Don't stop the traditions of showing me, telling me, holding me, hearing me," because that's what reassures her that her partner loves her. For men it often means, "Keep finding new ways to accommodate my practical needs and admire me, assist me, applaud me." Neither way is any more or less loving than the other. They are simply two different roads that lead to the same destination. Unless both people are willing to travel each of those two roads some of the times, one or the other may fail to experience the closeness he or she desires.

The way women described the intimacy they want is remarkably consistent. It's that sense of oneness between two people that flows in an open, meaningful exchange of thoughts, feelings, and affection. It's about each one entering the other's private world, not merely for a short visit but to unpack and take up residence. Women often see intimacy as something that includes physical displays of affection and time spent talking and listening to each other. But far more than that, intimacy is what gives women the feeling that they are no longer just "me" but also a part of "us." In fact, it's what defines the shared life. It's the whole bundle of visible and invisible ways her man assures her and keeps reassuring her that he is the one person on this planet who knows and cherishes her for who she really is. When something that precious is missing, women say they can't help but notice and respond. A woman will measure the strength of a relationship by how passionately and consistently the couple adheres to traditions they've established, such as saying, "I love you" before ending a phone call, kissing upon waking, exchanging secrets, or spending Friday night together no matter what. These personal rituals or a thousand others are the reassuring proof of real intimacy. So when her man becomes markedly less communicative or falters in performing those familiar and now expected traditions, it may signal to her that the relationship has stalled, if not derailed, or that there are deeper problems. For her, it's like a sudden drop back down to the bottom of the hill where no attachments have been established. The couple's trust, affection, and the sense of closeness that took time to develop is lacking. But it's not only the time that matters; it's also about what they can count on getting from each other and giving to themselves. They must focus on what their individuals needs are as well as their needs as a couple.

Ways to eliminate boredom:

+ Develop daily, weekly, and monthly rituals to nourish your love.
+ If you have kids, budget for a babysitter monthly so that the two of you can have a monthly getaway and focus on just the two of you.
+ Budget to attend a couples' retreat to reenergize your intimacy annually.
+ Have time away from each other, like girls' or guys' night out.
+ Practice not taking yourself too seriously in your relationship.
+ Mix up your social life together.
+ Show and cultivate genuine interest in each other. There is a lot to learn about each other after marriage.
+ Talk about the new things you are learning about each other each month.
+ Take care of yourself physically so that you will always have the energy to live passionately.
+ Strive to look your best at all times, like you did while dating.
+ Make a list of fun things to do weekly.

- Practice examining what drives the emotions behind your actions in the relationship.
- Add spontaneity in the relationship.
- Communicate with your partner that you want to break some routines and be more creative.
- Make it a point to touch your partner daily.
- Your relationship will survive by feeding it, watering it, and nurturing it. And it will grow.
- Remember to communicate, appreciate, and have fun.

Chapter 9
Laughter

A Daily Ingredient for Closeness

Laughter plays an important part in marriage because it allows couples to add the element that all relationships need: humor. People can respond to life in such a serious matter that it can cause stress, anxiety, depression, and other emotional problems. Everything in life can be perceived on such an intense level by people that it becomes imperative for them to stop and take a breather from all the stuff that goes on. Couples need moments to release some of the stuff, and what better way to do it than with laughter. In laughter, we can transcend our predicaments. We are lifted above our feelings of fear, discouragement, and despair. People who can laugh at their setbacks no longer feel sorry for themselves. They feel uplifted, encouraged, and empowered. We are often powerless against the events in our lives, and sometimes there is little we can do to stop the things that upset us. We can, however, *minimize* the hold that these things have over us by finding some humor in them. Humor can help smooth the rough edges of our day or the most trying moments in our life.

Humor helps us cope with difficulties in several ways. It instantly draws our attention away from being upset. Much of the suffering we experience is not a result of our difficulties but how we view them. It is not so much the actual event that causes us pain but how we relate to it. All of us experience life's traffic jams, fender benders, and roadblocks. For one person, the bus breaking down is a major upset, but for another, it is a glorious chance to enjoy one's surroundings while walking to one's destination. As scientists investigate the connection between the mind and the body, they are finding more and more evidence indicating that our feelings, thoughts, and attitudes not only play an obvious role in our mental health, but are also major contributors to both our physical well-being and our ability to recover from illness. Our daily stresses that go unchecked over a period of time seem to be the biggest culprits and probable perpetrators of physical and mental illness. These findings show that it is of vital importance that we use a positive attitude, with a healthy sense of humor, to aid us in reducing stressful situations, unexpected changes, and losses. This will prevent them from manifesting into physical and emotional disorders.

By focusing our energy elsewhere, humor can defuse stressful events. It releases built-up tension and pops the cork of such things as fear, hostility, rage, and anger. Fear and rage are two emotions that have been associated with heart attacks. Humor can play a major role in maintaining a healthy heart. Humor acts to relieve fear. Rage is impossible when mirth prevails. To have a sense of humor is to have an understanding of human suffering and misery. Humor bespeaks a sad acceptance of our weakness and frustration. But laughter also means freedom. We may not actually solve all our problems with others, but we may discover some relief, at least while we are laughing our way out of the situation. Whether it is an embarrassing situation, a minor upset, or a major setback, if we can see some humor in it, we begin to disconnect and free ourselves from that event. Adding humor to our difficult times can be one of the wisest things we can do to help us cope. It helps us stop worrying about problems and get on with our lives. Humor doesn't changes things permanently, but it makes everything okay for a while.

Humor approaches things sideways, upside down, backward, and inside out. When we can find some humor in being upset, it no longer seems as large or as important as it once did. Humor expands our limited picture frame and gets us to see more than just our problem. Like sheep that get lost nibbling away at the grass because they never look up, we often focus so much on ourselves and our problems that we get lost because we forget to stop and look up to see the larger picture. It is our sense of humor that provides a God's eye view of our situation.

We hear laughter in hospital waiting rooms, church sanctuaries, and funeral homes. These are not funny places. It is possible that some people actually laugh in serious situations or even at times when they're down in the dumps. Amazingly, many of us do. We laugh when we really need to just let the body do what comes naturally. Laughing at life's gloom is like screwing up your face to take medicine and finding out that it actually is not so bad. Laughter through tears has been called the perfect emotion. A society becoming more depressed needs a natural, effective solution to combat woes, and laughter is that solution. Everyone would be in less of a funk if they laughed more. Unfortunately most people tend to stop laughing when they feel really down; they stop doing anything emotionally. They don't laugh, they don't cry, they don't get angry. They are totally and miserably numb. People really need to connect to their feelings, and when we don't for any length of time, we become miserable. Feeling glum, tired, and generally negative, a common complaint into today's world, is the result of anger and sadness that we haven't allowed ourselves to acknowledge.

So, if you don't medicate your feelings with an antidepressant, what can you do to feel better? You can work at keeping yourself laughing. Laughter will release anger you may be holding in and causing that sick, negative feeling that's so hard to shake. It will clear your mind, lift your mood, and help you cope. Unfortunately, it will not change your problems or minimize their importance. It will, however, change you so you can deal with your problems and relate to them from a more realistic, less overwhelming perspective. It will also help you feel pleasure and fun once again.

You can fight that depressed feeling by forcing balance into your life. You can do this by adding pleasure in your daily actions. It's okay to feel as good as you can; you don't have to worry. The serious stuff will always take care of itself. If you reacquaint yourself with your ability to approach life in a spirit of play, you will laugh a lot more. Imagine that! All those heavy, serious things that are weighing you down will lighten up. Playing with painful things is a minor source for our laughter. As human beings, we know this deeply and instinctively, and we were all about that as children. All we have to do to regain this special human quality is grant ourselves permission to play and laugh.

Laughter is a birthright, a natural part of life that is innate. Infants begin smiling during the first week of life and laugh out loud within months of being born. Even if you did not grow up in a household where laughter was a common sound, you can learn to laugh at any stage in life. Begin by setting aside special times to seek out humor and laughter. Eventually, you'll want to incorporate humor and laughter into the fabric of your life, finding it naturally in everything you do. Anyone can join the laughter movement. All it takes is a willingness to risk some loss of control. The time may start with a few shy giggles. The courageous may jump in with deep belly laughter. A sense of humor is not required. There's more than enough stress to go around, and absurdity abounds in our daily lives. All you have to do is believe, let go, and clap your hands, and laughter will live again. So, will you let go? Laughter is feeling good, which allows us to live fully.

Humor is infectious. The sound of roaring laughter is far more contagious than any cough, sniffle, or sneeze. When laughter is shared, it binds people together and increases happiness and intimacy. In addition to the domino effect of you and amusement, laughter triggers healthy changes in the body. Humor and laughter strengthen your immune system. It boosts your energy, diminishes pain, and protects you from the damaging effects of stress. Laughter lowers blood pressure, massages our internal organs, works on our respiratory system, and eases tired minds. Best of all this priceless medicine is fun, free, and easy to use. Laughter in a relationship is a treasure. It is one of our primary reasons for even wanting a partner. All of us can see the magic power of laughter after we have a good belly laugh, and if someone offers us laughter as part of being with them, we tend to stay. Each time we laugh we feel better, our step becomes a little peppier, and we feel a little closer to the person we laughed with. The world seems brighter and friendlier, and we are able to approach things more positively. Laughter is a powerful antidote to stress, pain, and conflict. Nothing works faster or more dependably to bring your mind and body back into balance than a good laugh. Humor lightens your burdens and inspires hope, connects you to others, and keeps you grounded, focused, and alert. Everyone involved in a relationship cherishes the positive things that laughter provides. We all want to stay immersed in the love and laughter that brings us together. We want to keep the feelings that enabled us to join our lives together easily in joy, optimism, and love. Laughter helps you stay emotionally healthy. The ability to laugh, play, and have fun with others not only makes life more enjoyable, but also helps you face problems, connect with others, and be more creative. Life brings challenges that can either get the best of you or become playthings for your imagination. When you become the problem and take yourself too seriously, it can be hard to think outside the box and find new solutions. But when you play with the problem, you can often transform it into an opportunity for creative learning. Playing with problems seems to come naturally for children. When they are confused or afraid, they make their problem into a game, giving them a sense of control and an opportunity to experiment with new solutions. Laughing with others in playful ways helps you retain this creative ability. The body's healing system responds favorably to positive attitudes, thoughts, moods, and emotions (such as love, hope, caring, intimacy, joy, laughter, and humor) and negatively to negative ones (such as hate, hopelessness, pessimism, indifference, anxiety, depression, loneliness, and criticism). You want to organize your life to maintain as positive a focus as possible. There is no longer any doubt that your daily mood or frame of mind makes a significant contribution to your health—especially when it persists day after day and year after year. Anything you can do to sustain a more positive, upbeat frame of mind in dealing with the daily hassles and problems in your life contributes to your physical health at the same time it helps you cope with stress and be more responsive in your relationships. Your sense of humor is one of the most powerful tools you have to make certain that your daily mood and emotional state supports good health.

Human beings are not born serious, We begin life fully equipped with an innate playfulness and the ability to laugh freely. Sadly, we curb our playfulness and our laughter as a sacrifice to the serious business of adulthood. In order to keep laughing, we need to be in a partial state of playfulness, consciously or unconsciously. Laughter can help us ease our adult seriousness and retrieve that lost sensation of play. The fact that you feel better after a good laugh is enough for many to conclude that laughter must be good for you. But new evidence confirms what our grandparents knew all along. Your sense of humor not only enriches life, but promotes physical, mental, and spiritual health.

Ways to keep laughter and humor in your relationship:

+ Go to a comedy club at least monthly.
+ Try to help each other find some humor in everyday things you see.
+ Watch a funny movie together at least monthly.
+ Share a daily joke.
+ Point out the day's absurdities to each other.
+ Consciously smile at each other more.
+ Take turns being responsible for a humorous thought for the day.
+ Count the number of times you laugh each day, and share.
+ Tell each other how much you enjoy the other's laughter and sense of humor.
+ List the positive things that happened in your day and read them to each other.
+ Take turns doing something silly for each other daily.
+ Play together one hour a week. For example, sing, dance, race each other, give exaggerated hugs, or count smiling faces when driving together.
+ With children, create an environment where laughter is appreciated and encouraged.

Chapter 10
Personal Growth

A Lifelong Requirement for Your Relationship Journey

The potential of man and woman is limitless. We have been placed in a world of abundance. There is opportunity around every corner, and by making the right choices, you can't fail. Unfortunately, it is a fact that a great many people are unhappy in their relationships and their jobs. They go to work every day out of necessity, not because it is interesting or challenging. Each day they spend eight hours in misery with no room for personal growth. Personal success is only a flicker, and the fire is never able to ignite. This human trait flickers first, then waits for the right moment to become a blazing inferno, but the success challenges may be quenched in favor of family safety and security. The desire to succeed has to be a daily focus. There is a breed of unsettled people who strive for personal success and fulfillment. They strive for excellence in plotting their own course. They are an energized movement of movers and shakers and self-motivators who are always tuned in and turned on. They cut their teeth on challenging electronic games and computers. And they appreciate the opportunity and abundance that is provided for them. In their energized world there is no fear of success or failure. They live life to its fullest because in their hearts they know they are backed by infallible principles and laws. They're not afraid to show a mighty driving force. Their reward is a result of, and not a means to, how well they played the game. It's not benefits they seek, but the rush of the challenge.

The promise of promotions and recognition doesn't mean anything to these people; in fact they are more apt to move on because there is no stimulus for higher achievement. These are the people who climb mountains, race cars, and jump from airplanes. Success is not an option but a necessity. Some surrounding media contains negative influences at every turn, discouraging personal growth. Even though society stifles differences or anything not understood, people who know who they are aren't afraid of life, and disregard negative manipulation. These people are self-assured and do not cave in to the pressure of those who would see them fail. Self-assured people face life on the assumption that they will be successful. There is no maybe or perhaps—only doing. They know they must be precise in formulating a plan for success by acquiring knowledge and becoming as professional as possible and being persistent. They realize this is the price to be paid and are willing to pay it. They develop a desire that becomes the fuel that drives them toward better things and becoming well balanced in their life's functioning. Their family, religion, and the financial, social, and physical parts of their lives are balanced for continued growth. Like any living, growing thing, they know they must be in balance for optimum result. Focused thinking and setting goals means there are proper procedures that must be adhered to. Successful people also know that there are requirements and procedures to follow for successful personal growth. The groundwork must be laid before a firm foundation can be built, like a blueprint for building a house. A blueprint for personal growth must also be drawn up. Without a blueprint or guide, success is only wishful thinking and not responsible action. An organized plan for personal success may be applied when basic fundamental success principles and procedures are developed and understood. Just like learning the basics of walking or talking, personal growth success requires learning certain basics. A concise formula can be devised and implemented that will lead a person, step by step, to success. It would not be rational to think that there is only one formula that fits everyone. Self-motivation is self-induced, and there are no guarantees for sustaining its endurance. The fact is, no one can work at full capacity every hour of every day. In doing so, life would become an endless cycle of active periods broken with occasional rest periods. It is more desirable to maintain a balanced, structured approach to a work schedule with each action directed toward a final outcome. Through planning and sticking to your plan, you can minimize nonproductive time that might threaten to undermine your success. Truly, the more active you are, the more you want to get active, because it's human nature to be creative. When people aren't creative, they tend to lose some self-esteem, and lower self-esteem increases the chances for failure. The potential for success lies within you. You are the ultimate factor: no excuses, no recourse. You make it happen. God, man, your mama—none of them will do it for you. You have to take advantage of the abundance that surrounds you. By making intelligent, calculated choices you can maximize your success. The reason most people don't achieve success is that they don't have a clear, defined concept of exactly what success is in the first place. They won't take that first step because they don't know which direction to take; that's why most people opt to work for someone else. They simply don't want to deal with making decisions and they don't know how to plan. Personal growth affects every aspect of your life. As we evolve, we go through different stages of growth, and our ability to understand is determined by where we are in our growth process. From birth we learn to fulfill our most basic needs. As adults, we must learn to fulfill our higher needs— that is, we must discover our inner ability to fulfill all our adult needs. Successful people are those who understood that personal growth is more than possessions and money. People who think that personal growth is gauged by material wealth couldn't be more wrong. Successful people also give back. Success is fulfillment, happiness, and having meaningful and loving relationships. This necessitates balance, which increases fulfillment. Everyone has the potential to achieve their worthwhile, predetermined goals by simply planning to do so. There is one major thing that blocks our personal growth, and that is the stress that gets stored in our nervous system and our beliefs. Once we understand the value of personal growth and start to focus our attention on it, we must find a process for releasing the built-up stress that gets stored in our nervous system as children. As the stress is released, our awareness expands and we are able to see different possibilities.

We can change some of the old beliefs that have kept us from making the progress we dreamed for as kids. Personal growth is what an unlimited future is all about. Everyone must discover or create a process for releasing stress and strengthening their nervous system. The process may include breathing exercises, yoga, exercise, meditation, or focusing techniques. It is important that you work on the process daily. You must start from where you are today, and you will grow. As this personal growth takes place, your life will begin to improve and continue to improve as you move through higher and higher levels of growth. Also, there are some laws of nature or principles of life that govern our experiences. One of these principles is the law of attraction. This principle is always working, something like gravity. We attract to ourselves whatever we believe in and project to the world. Consequently, our beliefs in limitation will block our personal growth. And remember, your personal growth stops only when you die.

Things to do to enhance personal growth:

+ Develop a personal inventory of where your life is now.
+ Review where you want to be and why.
+ Ask the question, are you happy in your life now? Whether the answer is yes or no, ask yourself why.

- Develop a to-do list for things you have not achieved yet in your life, and get busy.
- List those things that make you feel good.
- Choose what's important and valuable to you in your life.
- Your journey to heal, improve, and grow starts from within.
- Do not use an all-or-nothing attitude.
- Try not to overgeneralize your thinking.
- Learn to feel what you actually do feel rather than what you "should" feel.
- Learn to say "I am sorry" with ease.
- Learn to forgive yourself for past mistakes.
- Learn to balance your personal life and work.
- Learn techniques to embrace dreams, aspirations, and lifestyle priorities.

Chapter 11
Things to Do for Marital Growth

Simple and Easy Steps to Follow

Newly married couples tend to take their first disagreement as a portentous omen. It is simply an indication that their personalities have not yet blended; it is not this first quarrel that determines whether a couple is happily married. Their happiness will depend upon how successful they are in blending their personalities to improve respect and love. When two people agree in their determination to let nothing get in the way of their developing a happy home, there is very little chance of them being disappointed. It must be realized, however, that such a state of affairs is not a simple coincidence but demands an active effort on the part of the husband and wife.

One golden rule that every married couple should observe is never to resort to deception. It is shortsighted to assume that a crisis can be avoided by trying to distort the facts. Deception will finally become apparent and undermine the absolute confidence that exists between the couple. A sincere apology, when indicated, does much more to ensure the respect and devotion of the spouse than does any attempt to ignore issues in the marriage. If you are focused on your spouse's faults, you will find them every time. But if you are set on finding your spouse's strengths, you will find them too. An old saying goes something like this: "Be to his or her virtues very kind. And be to his or her faults a little blind." In marriage, the husband and wife come together to build each other up. Envision how sweet your marriage can become if both of you focus on each other's positive qualities and build on them.

The Bible speaks of a husband and wife becoming one flesh. That means that couples do not lose their individuality but blend their personalities in a loving and intimate way. The choices you have made up to this point in your life have been a result of your attitude. Your attitude determines your actions, and your actions determine your accomplishments. The person you are and where you are today are the direct result of your attitude. Most people in bad relationships usually point to something other than themselves to explain their problems. But you can't rightfully blame your attitude on anything or anyone but yourself. You may not be able to control what happens to you, but you are completely responsible for your reactions to what happens to you. If you're in a relationship and love your partner and want your relationship to take on new meaning, begin right now and make a commitment to renew your love for each other. The kind of life I am talking about takes some extra work, but it is as simple as remembering how good it was when you first fell in love. Looking back at those good times is where your strength lies. It will help you renew your faith in love and open your heart to new possibilities. Look at why you chose that person in the first place. It will help you remember how much of a gift this person has been and how you may be taking his or her love for granted.

Remember, you are together to share your love with each other. A partner's love is a reminder that you are lovable even when you are not at your best. Never forget that a loving relationship not only brings two people closer, but gives both of you the courage to be your best in life. It is too easy to forget how to appreciate the person we love in our hurried pace through life. Love is one of life's greatest gifts to mankind, and yet many of us seem to forget how to enhance our belief in our dreams and ourselves. Never forget, real love lies deep within every one of us and only awaits our acknowledgment of it. Love is no mystery. Its results are magnetic in many forms. Love is the lamp that lights up our hearts. When we experience love of another, it makes us want to express our love for others in a myriad of ways. Our lives can be transformed by love. Our desire to know love draws us together. When we express our love, we touch the hearts of others meaningfully.

Knowing we are loved sustains our hearts and diminishes our difficulties. Love gives us the courage to be our best. Love cures. It cures those who give it and those who receive it. Love creates music from the disharmony of life's ups and downs, regenerating peace and joy. Giving love is like a song emerging from the beat of our hearts. Love promises us a life filled with magical moments. In romantic love, you transcend your daily experiences. That doesn't mean you leave the earth, but your daily life is infused with value not available without the presence of love. Colors are brighter. Sounds are sweeter. Winters are warmer. Nights are more secure. You perceive each other as a miracle and there is a magical fit like a glove. Your life together becomes erotic. All of life becomes more sensual, more attractive. Your energy and desire for living intensifies. You experience the fundamental connection between all living things. You bestow a special meaning upon each other, leaving room for no other romance in your heart. Your attraction is powerful, like magnetism. You want to be with each other, and everything you do together can feel romantic as long as you are connected and caring.

Ways to nurture marital growth:

+ Give what you want. If you want more love, offer love. If you want more affection, offer affection. If you want more intimacy, create an intimate environment.
+ Continue to create passion for life and for each other.
+ Respect each other's need for privacy and space.
+ Continue to build intimacy, both sexually and emotionally, throughout your marriage.
+ Sit down and make a list of what makes you feel loved and cared for. Read each other's lists and commit to doing the things on your partner's list.
+ Comfort, encourage, and affirm each other daily.
+ Never stop dating.

+ Apologize. In every conflict you play a part. Be responsible for it.
+ Remember, kindness toward each other is a great gift.
+ Take turns not asking your spouse to bring you something, get you something, find something for you, or serve you something. Instead, offer these things to your spouse.
+ Review and create new rituals for loving your spouse.
+ Celebrate milestones in your marriage.
+ Go on an annual or by-annual retreat to recharge your relationship.

Chapter 12
A Happy and Lasting Marriage

Fundamental Principles That Work

WHAT'S YOUR CHOICE?

The truth is that anyone, no matter how good the circumstances, can find a reason to have a negative attitude, and anyone, no matter how bad the circumstance, can find a way to maintain a good attitude. Your attitude toward life determines life's attitude toward you. How you think affects your approach to life's journey in a powerful way. What you believe about life determines how you perceive life, which determines what you receive from life. Nothing can stop a man or woman with the right mental attitude from achieving his or her goal, and nothing on earth can help the man or woman with the wrong mental attitude achieve his or her goals. When you have the right attitude, failure is neither fatal nor final; in fact it can be a springboard to success.

YOUR OPTIONS

People with a positive attitude focus their time and attention on solutions, not problems. Just about anybody can see problems; that doesn't take anything special. But positive people maintain a solution mind-set, seeing a solution in every problem and a possibility in every impossibility. Most of the things worth doing in the world were declared impossible before they were first done. Good marriages set goals just out of reach, but not out of sight.

LOVE REQUIRES CHANGE

If you don't change, you don't grow, and if you don't grow, you are not really living. Growth demands a temporary surrender of security. It may mean giving up some familiar but limiting behaviors, safe but unrewarding work, and values no longer working in a relationship that has lost its meaning. Taking a new step, uttering new words, is what most people fear most. The real fear should be the opposite course. The best way to ensure success is to start growing today. No matter where you may be starting from, don't be discouraged. Everyone who got where they are started where they were at.

REACHING YOUR FULL POTENTIAL

Growth today will provide a better tomorrow. Everything you do today was built from what you did yesterday. And all together, those things will determine what happens tomorrow. Find a way to put into action what you have learned about past relationships. Don't let your learning lead just to knowledge; let your learning lead to action.

LOVE IS FLUID

Whatever you do, don't allow yourself to stay on a plateau. Commit yourself to climbing the mountain of personal potential a little at a time throughout your life. It's one journey you'll never regret having made. Successfully married couples develop positive daily habits that help them grow and learn from each other.

LOVE HAS DIFFERENT SEASONS

Create a growth environment. Commitment to continual growth has its difficult moments as well as its rewarding moments. But there is a way to make the journey more enjoyable overall. You can live in a climate conducive to growth. Just as the growth of tropical fish is limited by the size of the aquarium in which they live, you are affected by your environment. If your current circumstances do not help you grow, you are going to have a hard time improving yourself and reaching your full potential.

FAITH IS ALL ENCOMPASSING

Feed your faith, not your fear. The bottom line is that you have a choice. You can feed your fears, or you can starve them. Both fear and faith will be with you every minute of every day. But the emotion that you continually act upon, the one you feed, dominates your life. Acting on the right emotion lifts you to success, whereas acting on the wrong one starts you on a disheartening detour.

AN ENDURING PRINCIPLE

Never withhold love. No matter how bad things get or how angry you are, never withhold love from your spouse. Sure, tell them how you feel. Acknowledge the problem. But continue loving your spouse and other family members unconditionally through it all. When you feel loved and supported by your family, you can weather any crisis. And you can truly enjoy success.

TALKING IS A GIFT

Develop platforms for communication. Be creative about finding ways to talk to each other. Take walks together. Call your spouse a couple of times during the day. Meet for lunch one day a week. Encourage honesty and transparency in conversations. Differences of opinion are healthy and normal in relationships. Never criticize or ridicule your mate. A common missing ingredient in marriages is dedication to making love work. Marriages may start because of love, but they finish because of commitment.

THE TOP OF THE MOUNTAIN IS IN SIGHT

Couples are to help build each other up where they have frailties. They are not called to change their differences. Couples are in each other's lives to encourage each other to become all God has in mind for them to be. If God has given you a marriage partner who seems very different from you, most likely he did so because your spouse has some gift, ability, or characteristic that you don't have but can use. You complement each other with your strengths and depend on each other to help in your areas of weakness. The basic need of all people is to love and be loved.

PAYING ATTENTION

God wants us moving forward, being productive, maturing from the challenges we face in life individually and as couples. Nurture a grateful heart in spite of your circumstances. Do not give in to complaining and a negative spirit. Say things to your spouse that will produce good fruit.

WHAT IS YOUR LIFE BUILT UPON?

Stay playful and open to God's instruction. Be in tune with his timing, recognizing the season you are in. Yield to the changes, and anticipate and prepare for the next phase of life. How and when you get to move on in love depends on how you respond to where you are right now in your relationship.

LOOKING INTO YOUR SOUL

Happiness is not a matter of events; it depends upon the tides of the mind and the heart. True giving, radiant giving, comes from the same inner place as deep happiness. Happiness is a desire to share our sense of worth and values with another person. It is having the self-esteem to feel that what we have to offer in a relationship is valuable. The manner in which we give love is a reflection of who we are. We have all heard it said that if you want something different to happen, you have to do something different. Change your approach in order to make the relationship run more smoothly and last longer. That's right: flip the script on your attitude, words, and actions. This is within your power. Are you working in conjunction with what God designed for you to do, or are you stubbornly trying to fit a different mold?

LOVING IN UNISON

Loving couples know that true happiness comes from a profound and enduring feeling of commitment, capability, and centeredness. It is a rich sense of well-being that comes from knowing you can deal productively and creatively with all that life offers, both the good and the bad. It is knowing your internal self and responding to your real needs rather than the demands of others. It's a deep sense of engagement, living in the moment and enjoying life's bounty.

WHEN YOU HAVE THE PRIZE

Loving couples are emotionally wired, regardless of the problems swirling around them. They move through life with a grace, warmth, and vigor that is alluring and mysterious. That is happiness. People grow and change and learn to make themselves happy. First, you truly can choose your happiness. It is not a matter of luck or happenstance. Happiness comes from within; you can't find it outside of yourself. You have the power to create your own happiness. In other words, when couples work as a whole, their total result is far greater than the sum of their individual parts. That synergy is what creates deep and long-term happiness. Appreciation is transformed into awareness and how we acknowledge our mates. It is the way we open our emotional floodgates and let our happiness flow into the world. Appreciation is our way of living fully in the moment. With appreciation, we move mountains, take what is ordinary and turn it into something special, elevate a friendship into a great relationship, disarm a business adversary, make a crisis more bearable, and balance sadness with beauty. How? By seeing what there is to appreciate in our mates. Your life was designed to be fruitful, productive, effective, joyful, and fulfilling. If any or all of these ingredients are missing, it is time to find out why. This usually requires exploring below the surface to see what is broken.

Chapter 13
Communication

You Can't Have a Meaningful Relationship Without It

Communication is something we all know is necessary to keep any relationship strong and loving. Although we are aware of the importance of communication, we still seem to be clueless about what exactly good communication is. This does not mean you are clueless as a person, but it does mean that more attention is required on your part. Become more open and invite the many forms of good communication, so that you will be able to understand yourself and your partner better. There is nothing that keeps a relationship healthier than understanding your communication style, as well as your partner's. Communication gives you the ability to work better as a team for your relationship. The first step in achieving better communication is to look at yourself first. People always tend to turn to their partner first when things are not running so smoothly in their relationship. They automatically start pointing out what their partner is doing or not doing, as well as how their partner is not listening to them. This may be true, depending on your situation, but it is important that you take responsibility for reviewing your own actions and first. Then you can point anything out about your partner. Remember, it is very easy to see other people's mistakes, but when it comes to looking at your own, it is much harder to accept criticism, even from yourself. Communication is not about who is right or wrong, but instead about helping each other see things from the other person's perspective. Then you can be on the same page and avoid any misunderstandings that may cause unneeded arguments.

Get winning out of your mind. Many couples claim to have tried communication techniques, but they do not always seem to work. If that is the case with you, then the best thing would be to slow down and take a few steps backward. If communication is not working in your relationship, look at what method of communication you are using. You see, communication itself cannot be the problem or the ineffective ingredient. Communication is the main key to a healthy relationship, so the problem must be the way in which you and your partner are communicating. When you and your partner talk to each other, do one or both of you talk to win the argument or do you try to reach a level of understanding about each other's needs and wants? It is very common for people to focus on being right and trying to persuade their partner to see things their way instead of just sharing what they think and feel so their partner can understand what they mean and what they need. Listening is crucial if you truly wish to have good communication. Are you really listening to what your partner is saying to you, or are you waiting to get things off your chest and make your point? Listening may sound like an easy enough thing to do, but many confuse it with sharing. Hearing what your partner is saying versus listening to them is indeed very different. Listening involves true dedication and giving your full attention to the words your partner is saying to you, as well as the tone and expression that go along with the words. Listening means that you are interested in learning more about what your partner is making an effort to tell you and making the emotional connection needed to achieve your relationship goals together. Keep in mind that when in a relationship, all communications between partners has to be open, honest, and nonjudgmental. This is important to maintaining a happy, healthy relationship. Communication is not so complicated once you understand the right way to communicate and, of course, the methods of communication that work for you and your partner. Effective communication cannot happen on its own or with the efforts of only one person. Both you and your partner have to be open and willing to work as a team on improving the way you communicate. You both can enhance your relationship skills and build a relationship where you both have an understanding of who you are as individuals and what you both need and want in the relationship. Remember to stay real with yourself and avoid painting a foggy and false picture of yourself. When communication goes wrong, it goes very wrong, but when it goes well, there is peace and harmony. Why does communication seem so hard for some? What makes good communication in a relationship and how is a higher realm of understanding actually achieved? Remind yourself from time to time that the way you communicate with the love of your life should reflect and reinforce how deeply you love him or her. Really, it's not a riddle at all but a very simple principle. Communication infiltrates every aspect of your life. It is the way you bond with others, exchange ideas, and convey your beliefs. Prehistoric man communicated, albeit with grunts, hand signals, and the occasional blunt force to the head, but he got the job done. Communication is a primal urge to connect with another person. It is the basic building block of what makes humans beings tick. Sharing is caring, after all. Communication can be clear or vague, open or guarded, honest or dishonest. It can even be spoken or unspoken, but there is no such thing as noncommunication. In fact virtually everything we do in the company of others involves communication. Our body language, facial expressions, tone of voice, and level of interest (or disinterest) communicate something to a perceptive observer. Because our ideas and interests are transmitted to other people through the way we communicate, we are more apt to get our needs met if we are effective communicators. The problem is that often we think we're communicating one thing but are actually communicating something quite different. At times we communicate so poorly that no one quite understands what it is we're trying to say.

Men and women have different communication styles. Men and women express communication differences in content, style, and structure. What do men and women talk about? Men often talk about sports, money, and business. Women most often discuss people, feelings, and relationships. Men often express themselves to fix a problem or converse for competition. Women most often express themselves to understand, converse to support, and talk to connect. How do men and women talk? Men typically use precise words that are to the point, without descriptive details. Women are more detailed, apologetic, and vague. Men's and women's body language is also different. Whereas women typically use nonverbal communication directly, men use it indirectly. Women stand in proximity to each other, maintain eye contact, and gesture more frequently. Men hold their distance, rarely establish eye contact, and gesture less dramatically. Men and women also handle conflict differently. Whereas women avoid conflict to ensure closeness, men use conflict to gain status.

Conflict is a part of life. It exists in almost all relationships, but it is not necessarily a bad thing. In fact, a relationship with no apparent conflict may be unhealthier than one with frequent conflict. Conflicts are critical events that can weaken or strengthen a relationship. Conflicts can be productive, creating deeper understanding, closeness, and respect. Conflict can also be destructive, causing resentment, hostility, and divorce. How the conflicts get resolved, not how many occur, is the critical factor in determining whether a relationship will be healthy or unhealthy, mutually satisfying or unsatisfying, friendly or unfriendly, deep or shallow, intimate or cold. Conflicts run all the way from minor, unimportant differences to major problems. There are conflicts of needs, wants, preferences, interest, opinions, beliefs, and values.

Healthy conflict resolution is easy to understand intellectually, but not as easy to apply and use consistently. It does, however, become easier once trust is developed. Both partners must view their conflicts as problems for them to solve. It's not about getting the best deal for me but about finding the best solution for us.

Couples must actively participate and make the commitment to work hard together to find solutions that are fair and acceptable to both. If you can avoid communication breakdown, you can make sure your relationship won't die. A breakdown in communication is the root of all problems in relationships. There are many signs that indicate the communication has gone south. Here are some signs to pay attention to:

+ Recurrent arguments/complaints (Perhaps you have not been true to yourself about what you want in the relationship. Or perhaps you only pretended to be okay with the outcome of what is still an unresolved issue.)
+ No complaints/too happy (You are lying to yourself and setting yourself up for disappointment. Don't expect people to change if you haven't told them what you want.)
+ Break in routine (You are telling yourself that something needs to change.)
+ Out-of-the blue issues (You were not honest with yourself about an issue that was resolved or you have formulated a thought after the fact that may not be accurate.)
+ Not talking (You have lost your interest in talking with your partner.)

Unfortunately signs of a communication breakdown are not always obvious. If you can spot issues early on, the relationship has a good chance of going the distance. Some communication problems are inevitable. Being able to recognize issues is half the battle. The other half is understanding and working to resolve the communication differences. You should be willing to talk about them and get relationship help if necessary. Also, because of earlier experiences in life, you each formed different feelings about how to approach situations in life. Many of the feelings you don't even realize you have until something or someone (such as your spouse) stimulates them and they come to the surface. Then look out ... Conventional wisdom says that good communication can improve relationships, increase intimacy, and build trust. The converse is also true: poor communication can weaken bonds and create mistrust. When you understand the importance of how maturity works in making love and marriage last, then you become a student of marriage. It won't hurt to pray and ask God to help you learn how to use your differences to work for you both. God created the different parts of the body, and they work together to sustain life!

Ways to avoid communication problems and build a strong, loving relationship:

+ Communicate without blame.
+ Listen generously.
+ Speak without arguing.
+ Focus on appreciation.
+ Turn your complaints into requests.
+ Shift from blame to wonder.

+ Ask for what you want.
+ Show your partner what you want to receive.
+ Learn to negotiate.
+ Learn to modify what you want.
+ Learn your partner's communication style.
+ Learn to speak up and not hold anything in.
+ Do *not* be defensive.
+ Do not stonewall discussions about topics that your partner wants to discuss.
+ Learn to read body language.
+ Look for signs of nervousness or stress when discussing important issues.
+ Watch for changes in mood and attitude.
+ Try to be specific rather than general about how you feel.
+ If you have mixed feelings about something, say so.
+ Learn to separate feelings from thoughts.
+ When expressing anger or irritation, first describe the specific behavior, then your feelings.
+ Avoid being judgmental.
+ Never think about winning an argument or discussion, because the relationship will lose.

Postscript

Each of the thirteen chapters in this book has been carefully constructed in the most beneficial way possible to help people enhance their marriage and raise questions and give answers that will improve each person's understanding of self. *Self* refers to one's emotional, physical, and most of all spiritual self. In reaching a state of self-awareness, you will begin to know your internal power. Your intuitive nature will grow, your sensitivity will be unleashed, and your world for love will open up. Life will become more enjoyable and fun as you learn to use your power, and your life will become more and more fulfilling. The path you walk will be rich with many treasures, as yet unseen. Unleashing your power gives you the insight to recognize these treasures and to know your higher lovable self. Your sense of self will grow, as will your self-esteem and your confidence. You will become more creative and more self-assured, and will know your strengths. These are just a few of the benefits of owning your own power to love. And remember, true commitment isn't expressed in an occasional "I love you" or in an anniversary card; rather, it's a constant awareness of a sacred process you and your partner have entered into together to experience the joys and lessons that love has to offer. This high commitment is reflected in every moment of every day of your relationship, in the way you listen to each other, the way you touch, the way you give, and the way you receive love. It transforms mere partnerships into special unions and fills your every action with meaning. When you have the privilege of making this kind of complete commitment, you have truly given yourself a wondrous gift of love.

Any good and loving relationship requires lots of hard work. The following list is one way for you to identify issues to discuss and explore together. Sometimes people don't know what questions to ask their partner to learn more about them. This is just a partial list. You can make up your own. Just remember to be honest and open with your partner, because your views and moods will change as the relationship grows and is enriched with each passing day.

THINGS TO DO:

+ Make a list of all the things you did not like that your parents said or did to you as a child and adolescent, including tone of voice and body language.
+ Make a list of twenty-five things you will do for personal growth.
+ Make a list of twenty-five things you will do for marital growth.
+ Make a list of seventy-five fun things that you would like to do in your life (fantasies included, individually and as a couple).
+ Make a list of five married couples you know and talk with who have a balanced relationship.
+ Make a list of your expectations in your marriage.
+ Make a list of your push-button issues.
+ Make a list of how you will meet the expectations of your mate.
+ Make a list of the fifty qualities you looked for in your partner five years ago and still look for today.
+ Make a list of the twenty-five qualities you bring to the marriage.
+ Make a list of things that could change your mood, positively or negatively.

+ Make a list of things that annoy you.
+ Make a list of daily affirmations that you can say to your spouse.
+ Make a list of fifty different ways that you can show your appreciation and affection for your spouse.
+ Make a list of the things that helped to change your views and behavior ten years ago and five years ago (that is, what caused you to look at things differently and act differently in relationships).

About The Author

Matthew D. Jones Jr., LMSW, ACSW, is an educator, mentor, motivator, and relationship coach. He is in private practice and specializes in working with couples. He has developed and facilitated many seminars on relationship building, premarital counseling, and marital stability. He is an Adjunct Professor of Clinical Social Work at Marygrove College and Wayne State University, and the author of two other books, Will The Real Black Men Please Stand Up and Raising Boys to Become Responsible Men. He lives in Detroit, Michigan.